FLORENCE GRISWOLD: THE KEEPER OF THE ARTISTS

by

Deb Adamson

Illustrated by: Anne Zimanski

FIRST EDITION

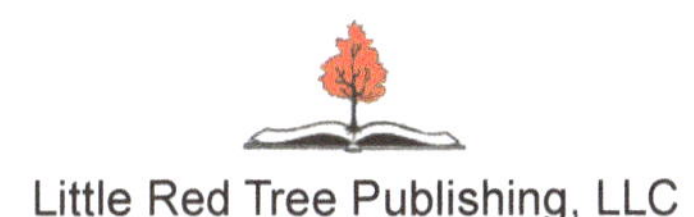

Little Red Tree Publishing, LLC

Printed and bound in the USA

Layout and Cover Design: Michael Linnard, MCSD
Fonts used in this book: Times New Roman, Charlemagne Stad, Arial, Trajan Pro and Gill Sans MT.

First Edition, 2019, manufactured in USA
1 2 3 4 5 6 7 8 9 10 LSI 24 23 22 21 20 19

Hardback: ISNB: 978-1-935656-60-9
Paperback: ISNB: 978-1-935656-61-6

All illustrations by Anne Zimanski, and photography on back page.

Photography of Deb Adamson on back page supplied by author.

Author's Note:

While the majority of this story is based on the facts we know about Florence Griswold, some of her childhood has been fictionalized. For instance, we don't know if Florence had any pets when she was young.

I made the presumption from her welcoming and generous love of cats and dogs as an adult, that she had a similar childhood affinity.

A sincere thank you to the staff at the Florence Griswold Museum for generously taking the time to review this manuscript.

Little Red Tree Publishing, LLC
635 Ocean Avenue, New London, CT 06320
website: www.littleredtree.com

Dedication

To Zach: “For all the treasured memories visiting the Florence Griswold Museum together.”

Love mom

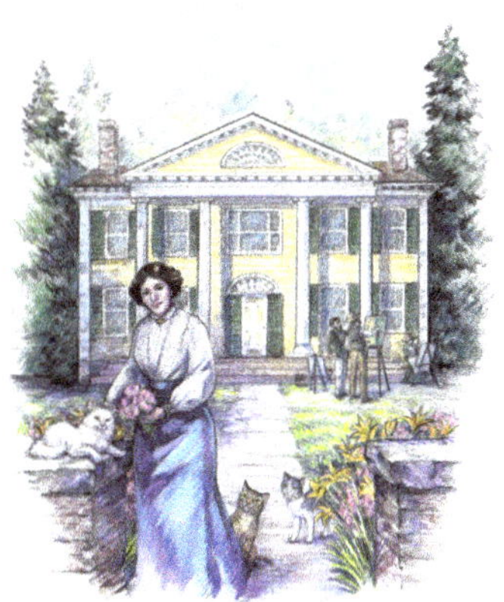

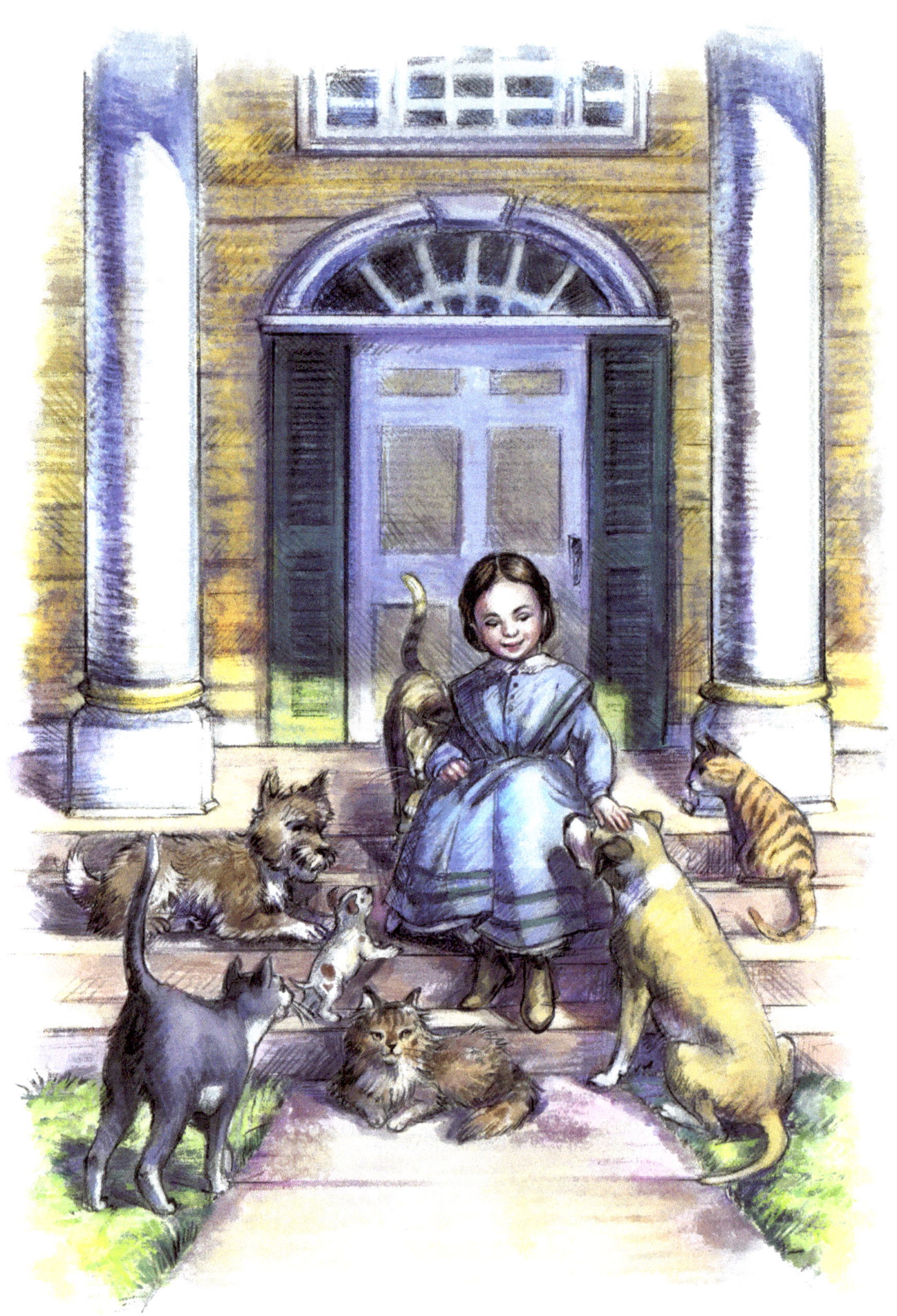

In a bright yellow house, in a small New England town, lived a young ship captain's daughter named Florence.

From what we know of her as an adult, it's easy to imagine that young Florence must have had a heart, big, wide, and welcoming. It's also easy to imagine that she invited into her home, any stray cat or dog, maybe even two or three at a time. But in reality we only know the following facts about Florence Griswold's childhood.

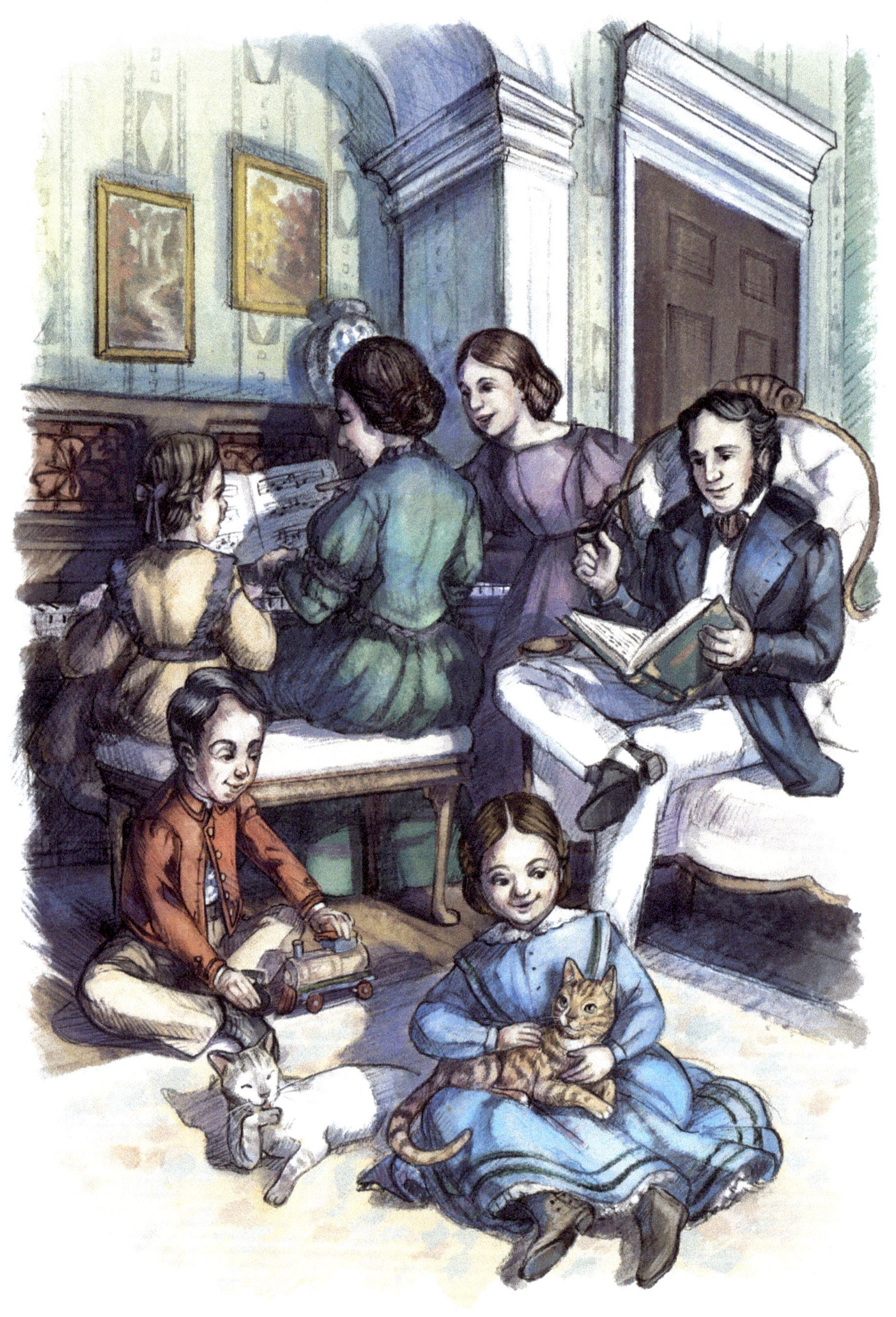

Florence lived with her mother, father, two sisters and one brother in one of the grandest houses on her street.

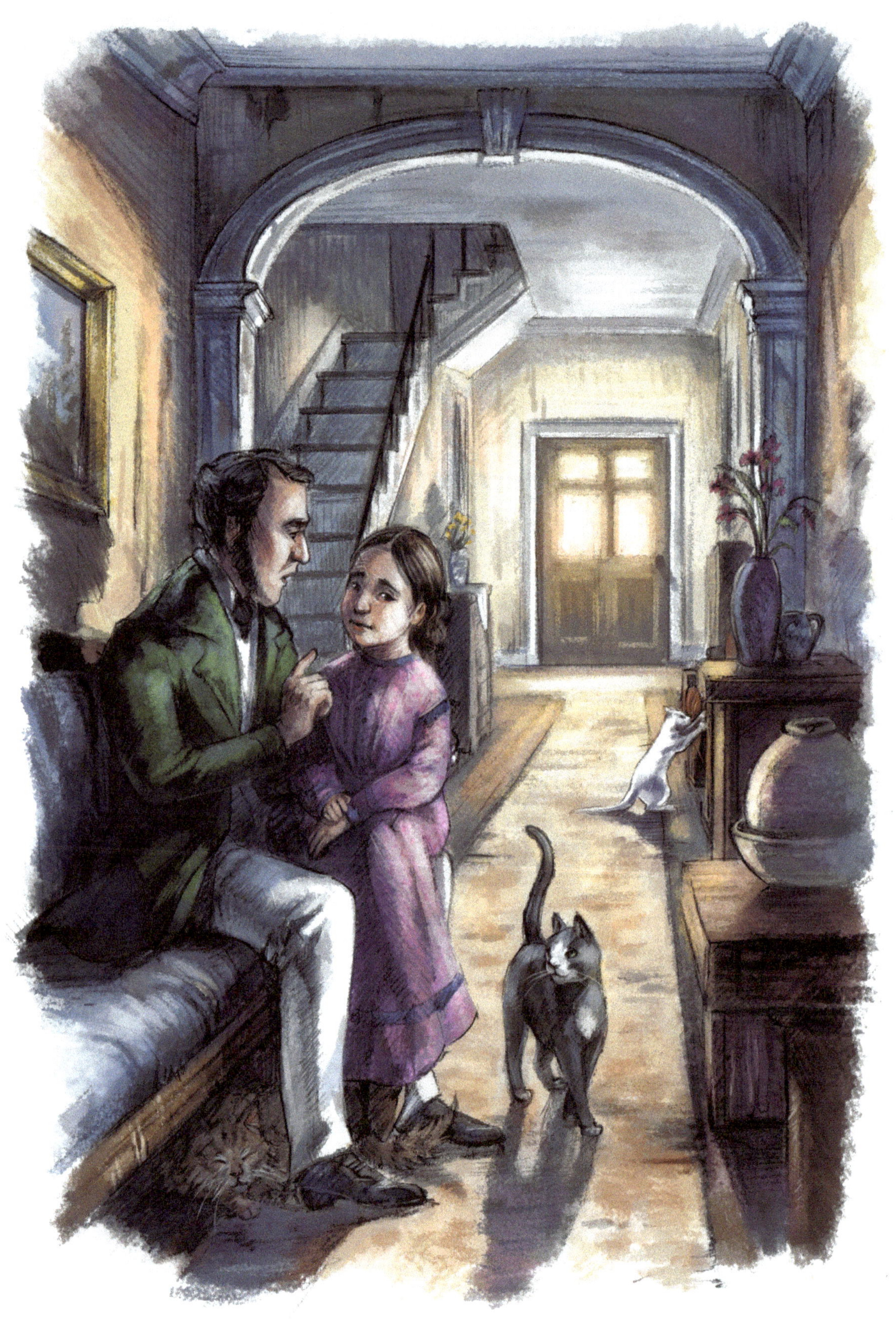

Florence's father, Captain Robert Griswold was a successful ship captain sailing between New York and London. But as time marched on, sailing ships fell on hard times. And so did the Griswold family.

In order to make ends meet, Florence's family was forced to turn the house into a girls' school.

"Florence. No more cats," said her father. "We have far too many mouths to feed as it is." But Florence whose heart was very big, wide, and welcoming, just couldn't abide by turning any away.

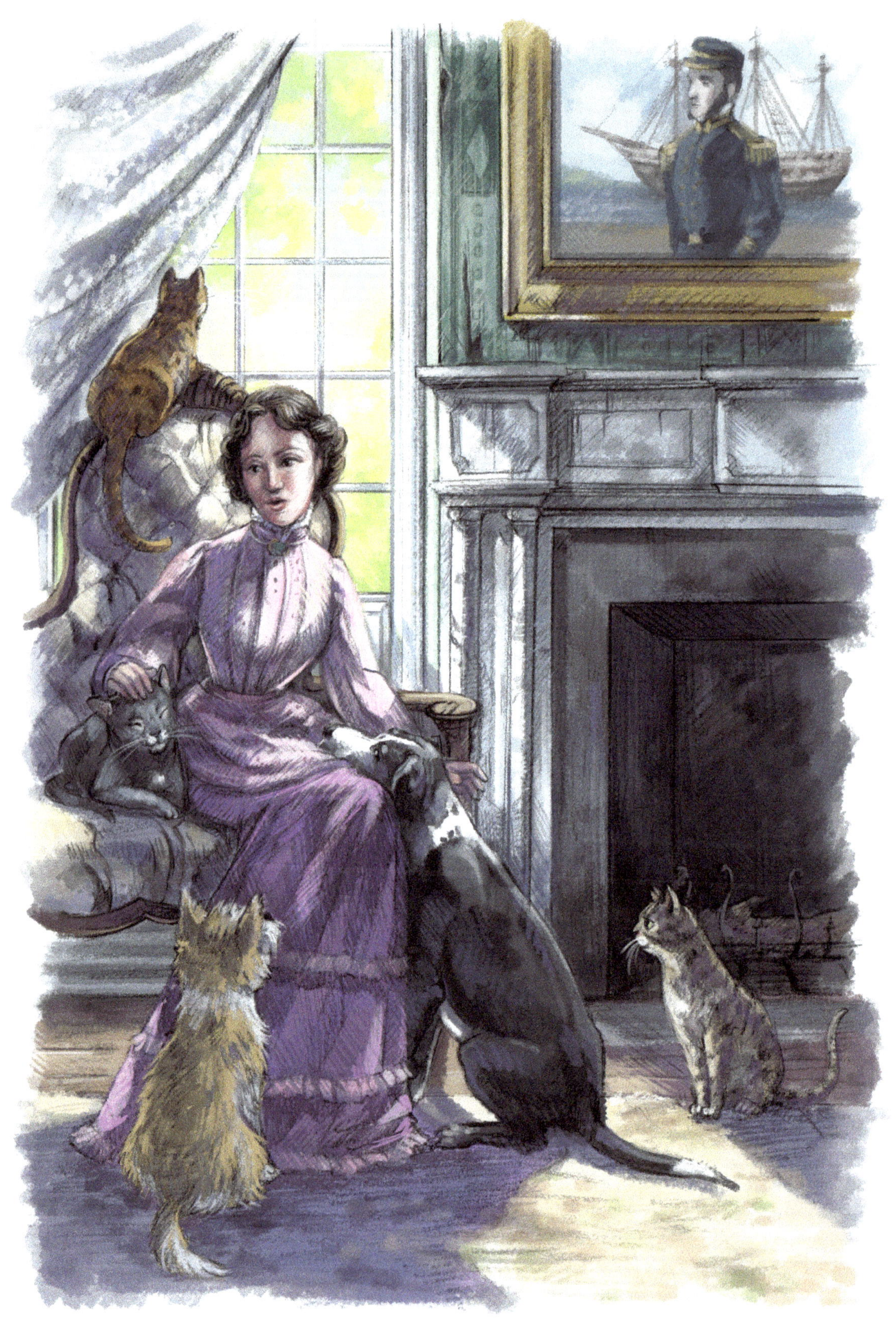

Many years later, when all of Florence's family had left and she was a grown woman, she found herself alone. Alone, that is, except for the company of her many cats and a dog, two or three. "What to do, what to do? Things are quiet and falling down around our ears," she said to her furry companions.

Since Florence had a heart so very big, wide and welcoming she came to the only plan that made sense. "We will invite travel weary boarders in and show them all the comforts of our home."

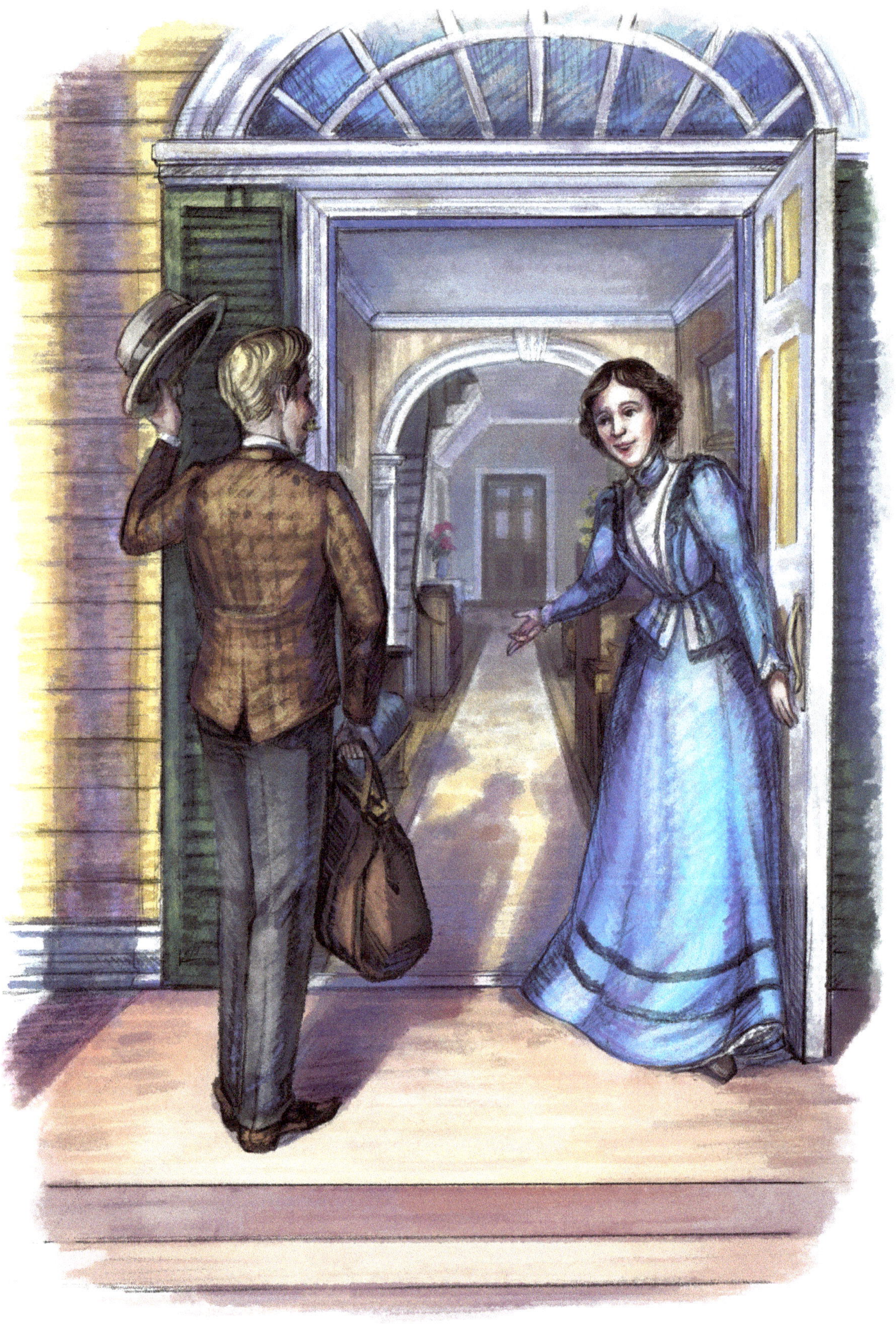

At first, a few visitors arrived in the summers from nearby New York City, Hartford, and Boston. But these passing guests hardly paid enough to keep food on the table, let alone pay for the upkeep of the run-down house.

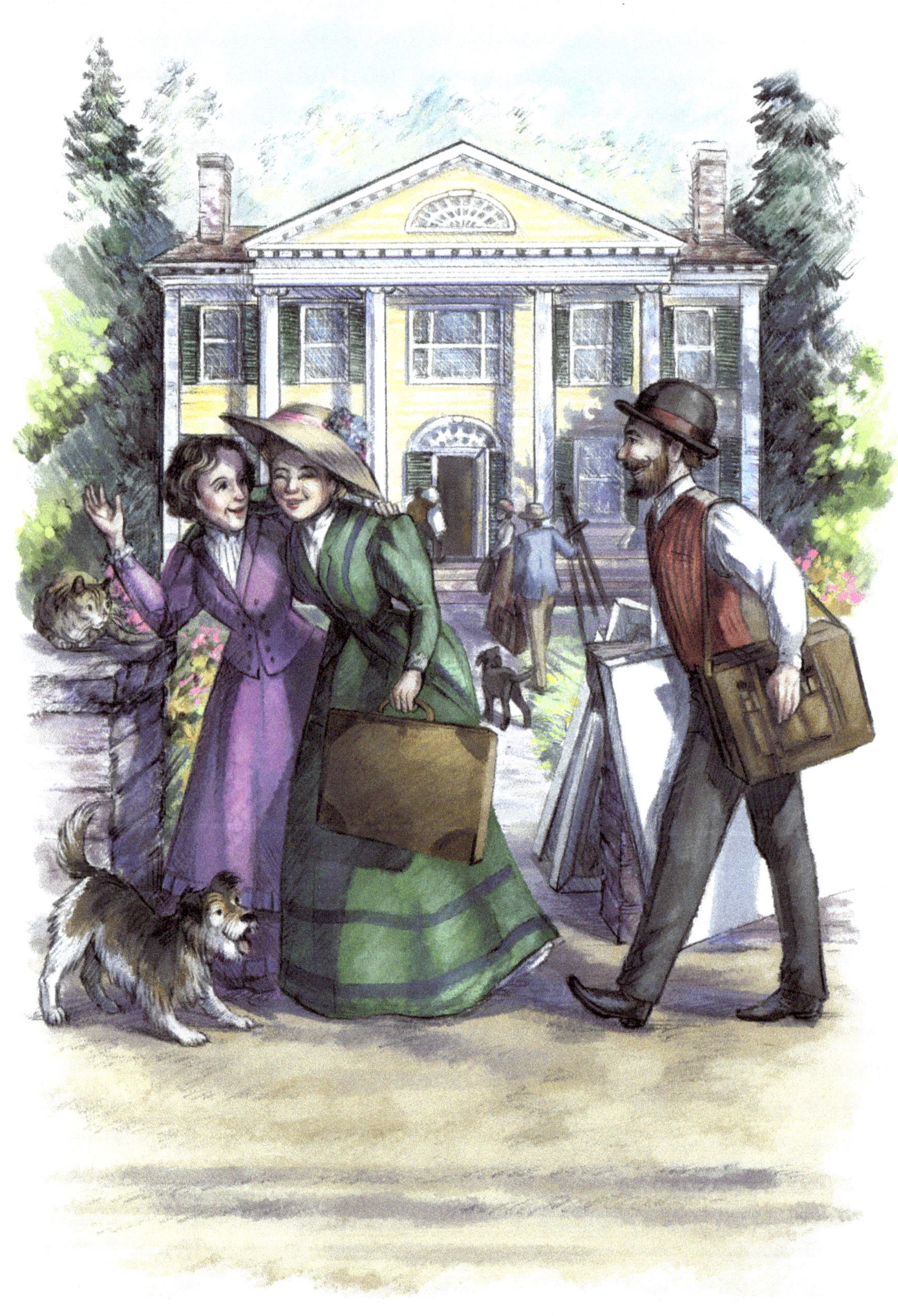

Then, one summer day, by chance Florence's luck changed. Artist Henry Ward Ranger came along scouting out the perfect place to set up an artists' colony. Ranger saw Miss Florence's home and immediately knew he had found the right place. Not only were the surrounding landscape, trees, and home perfect but Miss Florence, as he called her, radiated an irresistible warmth and kindness.

Years later when another artist, Childe Hassam arrived, the Griswold House gained even more popularity. It became known as the most famous Impressionist Art Colony in America.

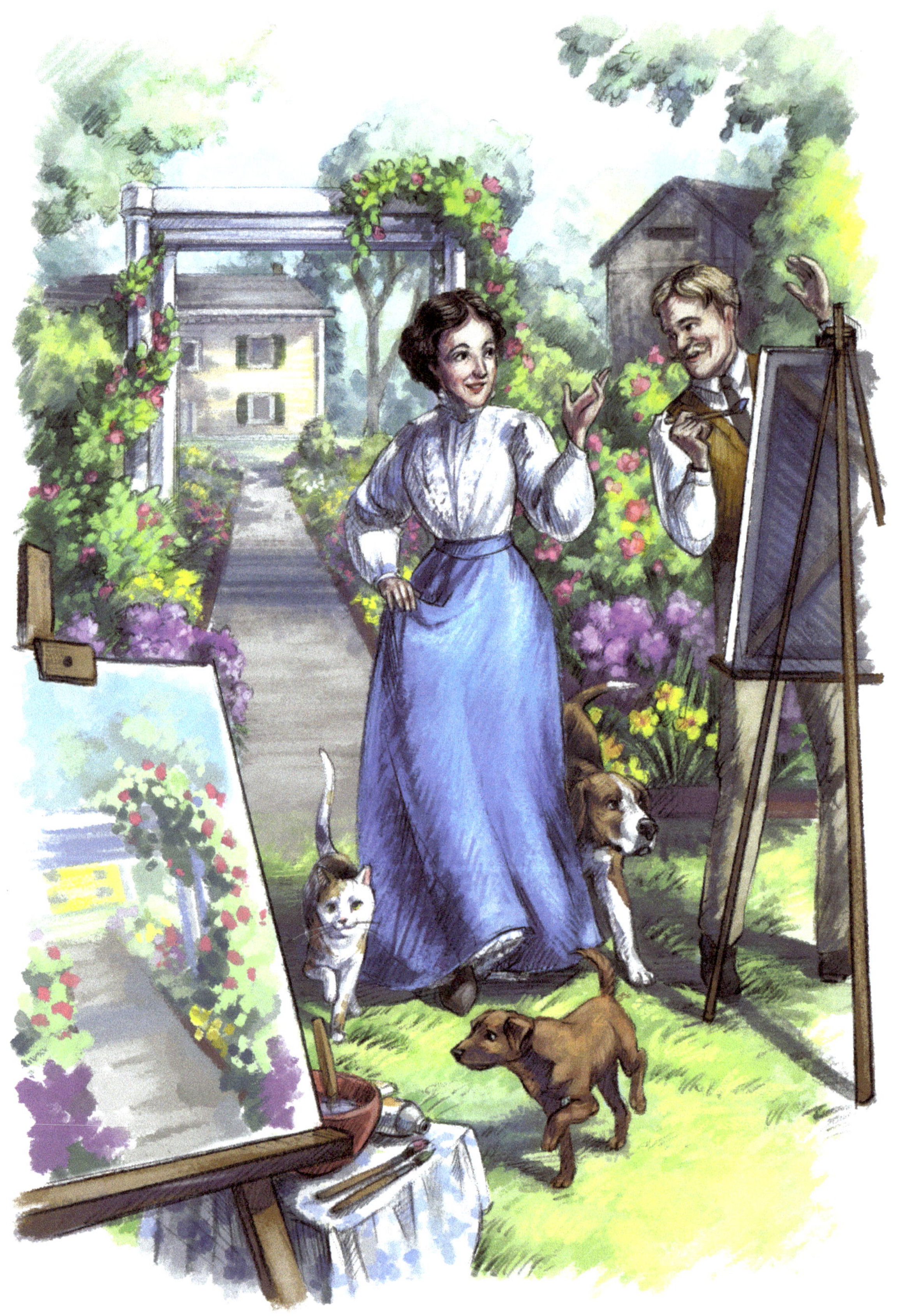

Despite all that fame, because Florence had a heart so big, wide, and welcoming, she only raised the rent once, in 1910. By making small home improvements to ensure her boarders were more comfortable, she went further and further into debt. And so the house continued to grow more and more tired. Yet, all the while she built strong bonds with her "Boys" as she called the artists.

As soon as the artists arrived weary from the train journey she helped them get ready for their summer of work. She'd unpack art supplies. Then set up easels on the grounds. She encouraged them as they painted the scenes that lured them—grazing cows and sheep, salt marshes, arched wooden bridges, and the distant white spired churches. Sometimes one of Florence's many cats and dogs made it into a painting. The artists spent their summers working hard on their creations.

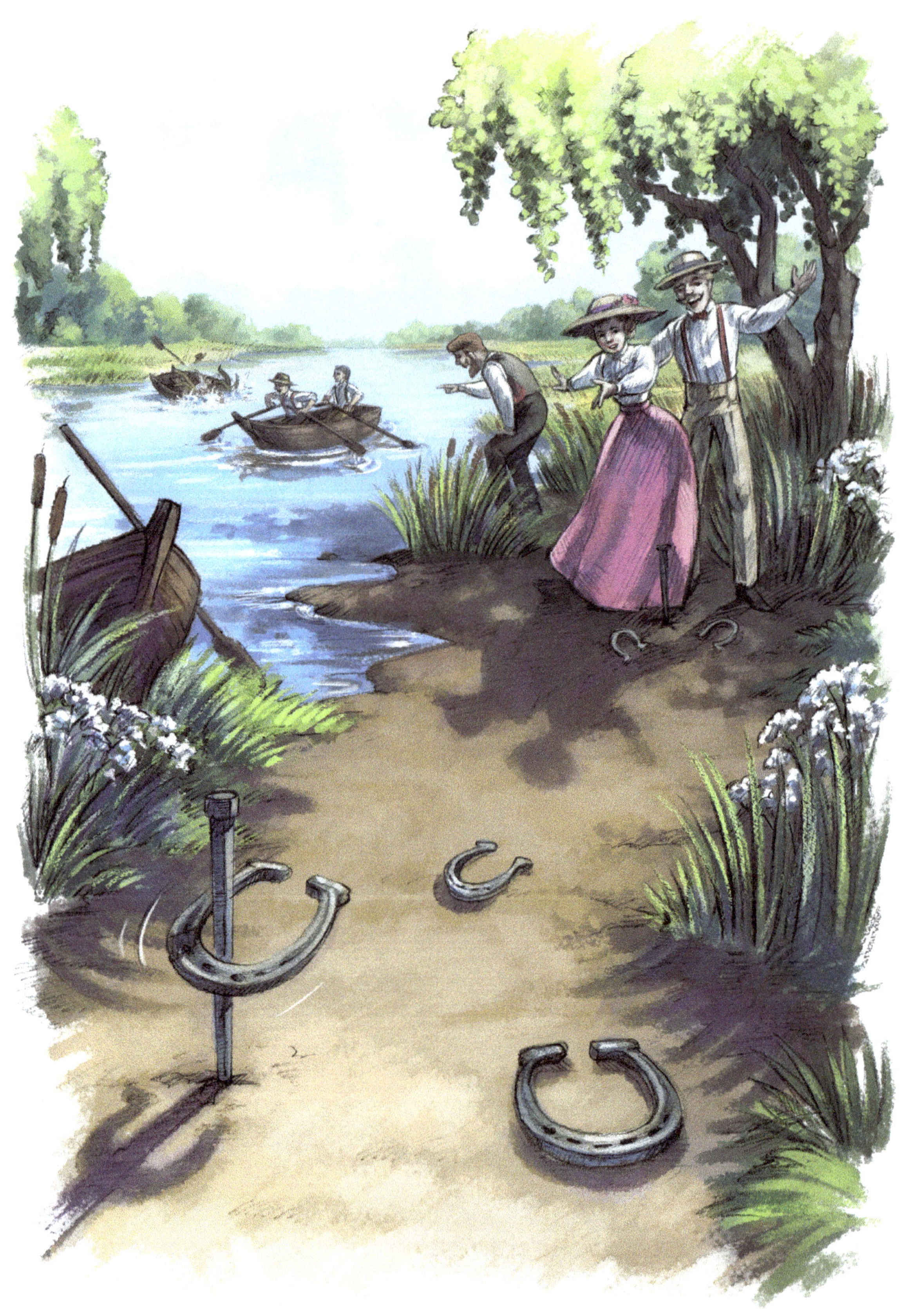

However, The Lyme Art Colony was not all work and no play. Miss Florence encouraged the artists' summer-camp like antics of playing baseball, horseshoes, rowing, and races down to the water and back.

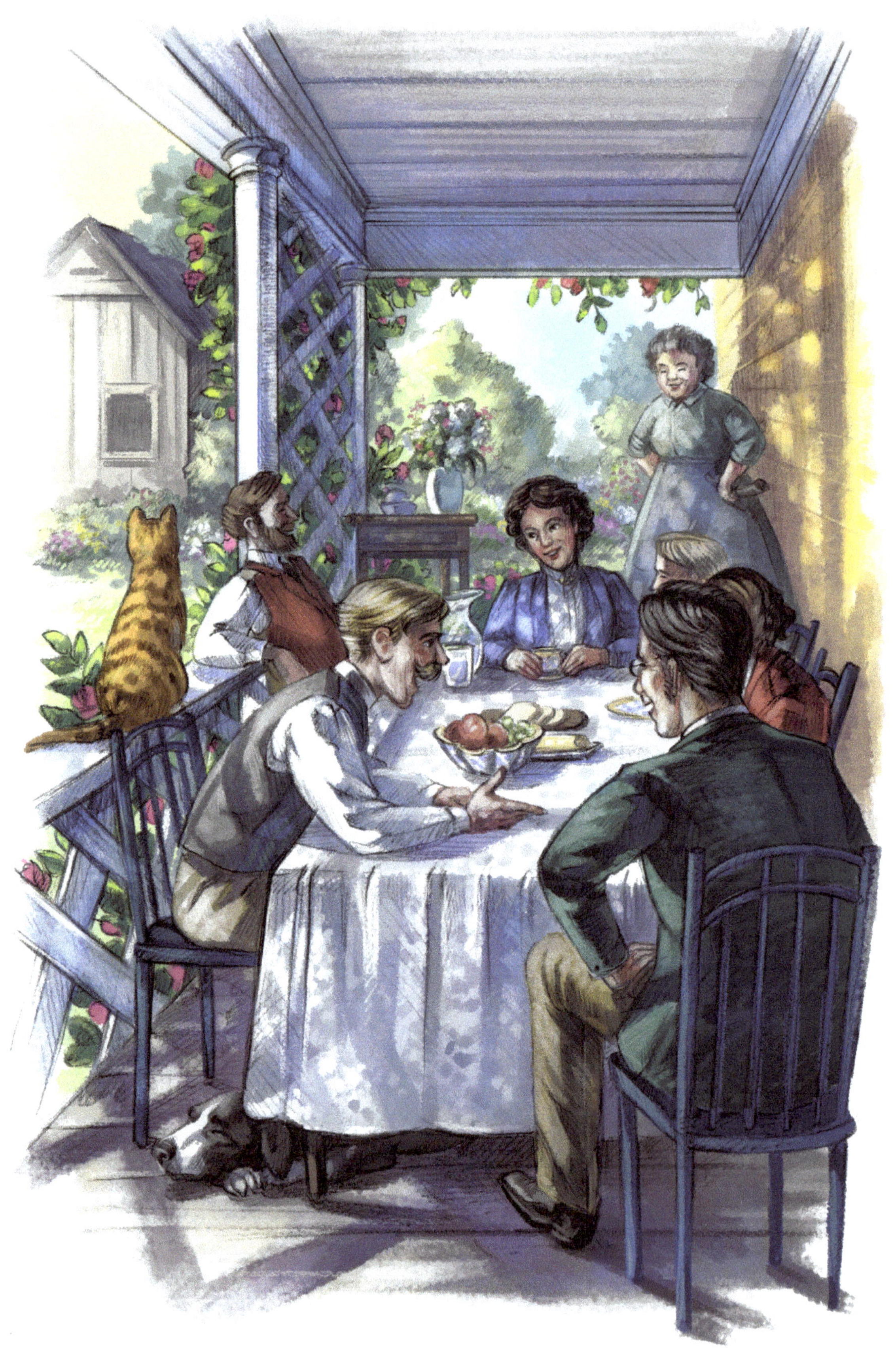

She especially enjoyed their company at mealtimes. Everynight Miss Florence's cook, Barefoot Mary, called the artists from their easels with her giant tinhorn. They feasted out on the porch on roasted turkey, ham, and beef.

They enjoyed fresh vegetables and herbs from Miss Florence's gardens. Dessert was usually a pie baked from the fruit orchards just beyond the garden. Underfoot, a dog and cat, two or three, were always hoping for a handout.

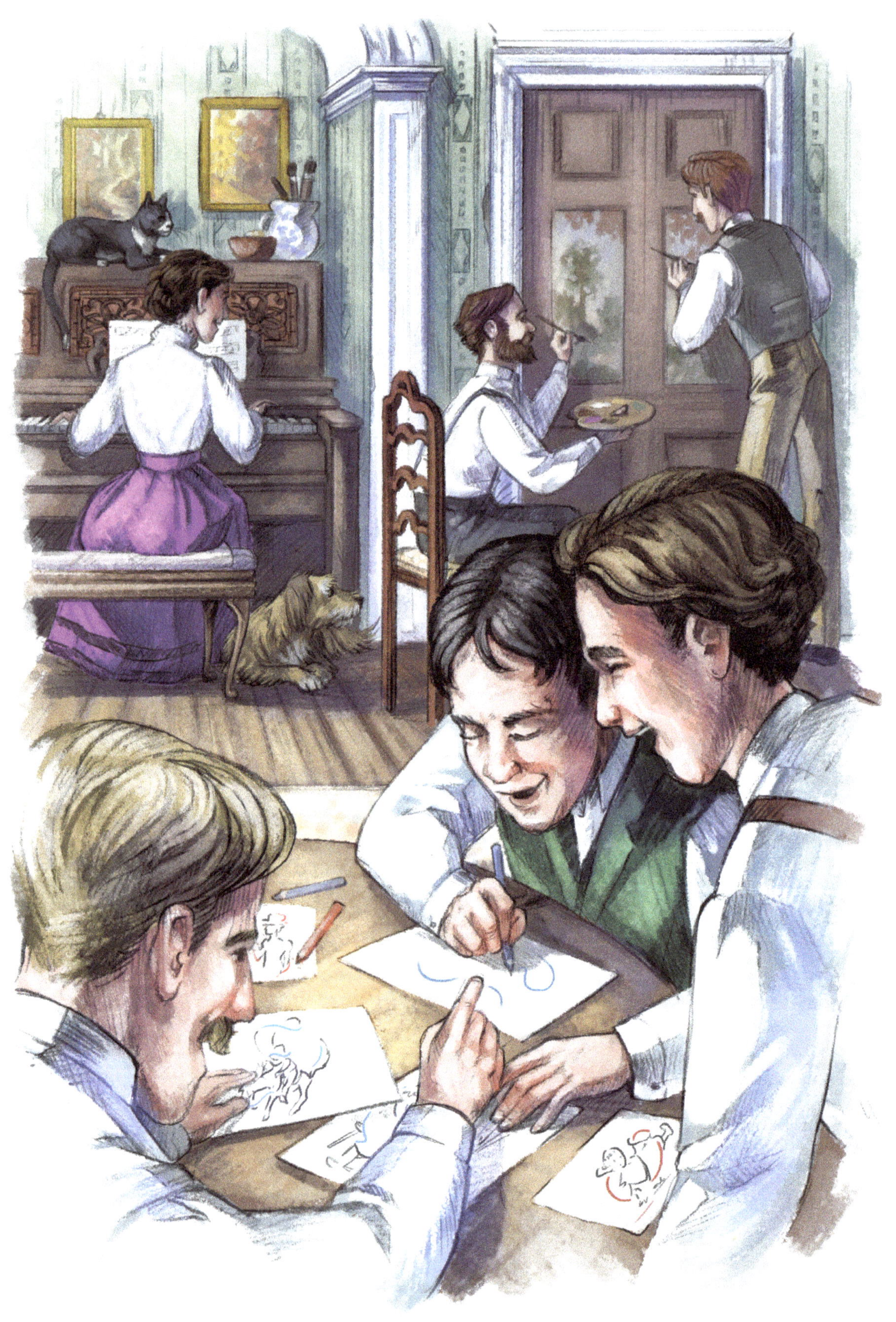

Later at night is when the fun really began. Miss Florence played piano, the artists then got busy with their antics taking turns at charades, card games, and critiquing each other's work.

A favorite game was the Wiggle Game, where one artist drew a few wavy lines and another took over from there. Laughter always echoed from the open windows. As the night wore on, artists got busy painting works right on the door panels and walls—forever gifts for Miss Florence, their hostess who had a heart big, wide, and welcoming.

The artists filled Miss Florence's heart like the full moon that glistened on the Lieutenant River behind her home, beckoning them back to the "Holy House," as the artists called it. Always as the weather turned warm.

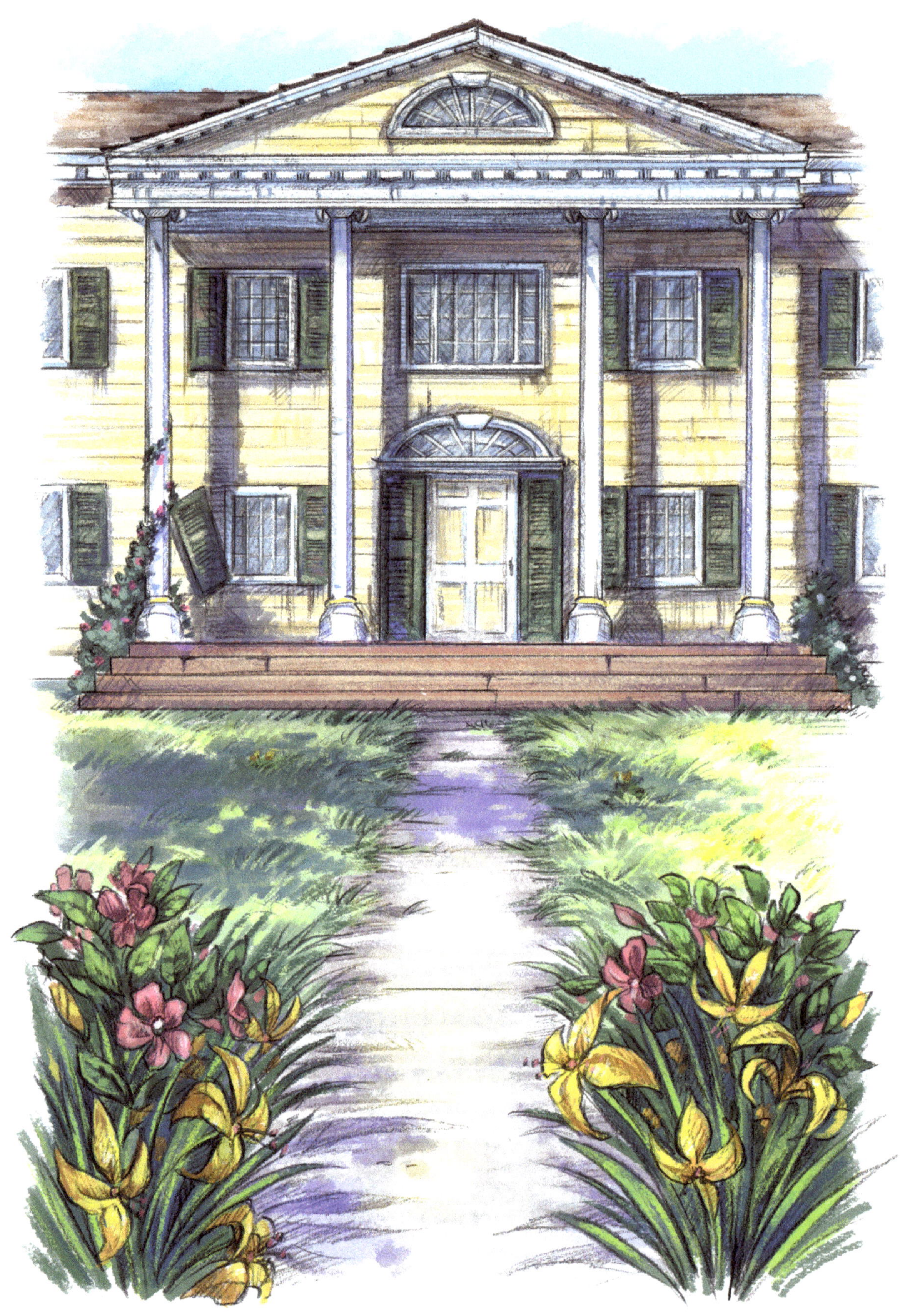

But as the years marched on, Miss Florence's generosity started to take its toll on the Griswold House. Because she charged her artists a pittance and often took credit out of the goodness of her heart, she could hardly make ends meet.

The Griswold House told the tale. The paint peeled inside and out. The wallpaper curled. Plaster cracked. Carpets grew worn. And the furniture sat broken and threadbare.

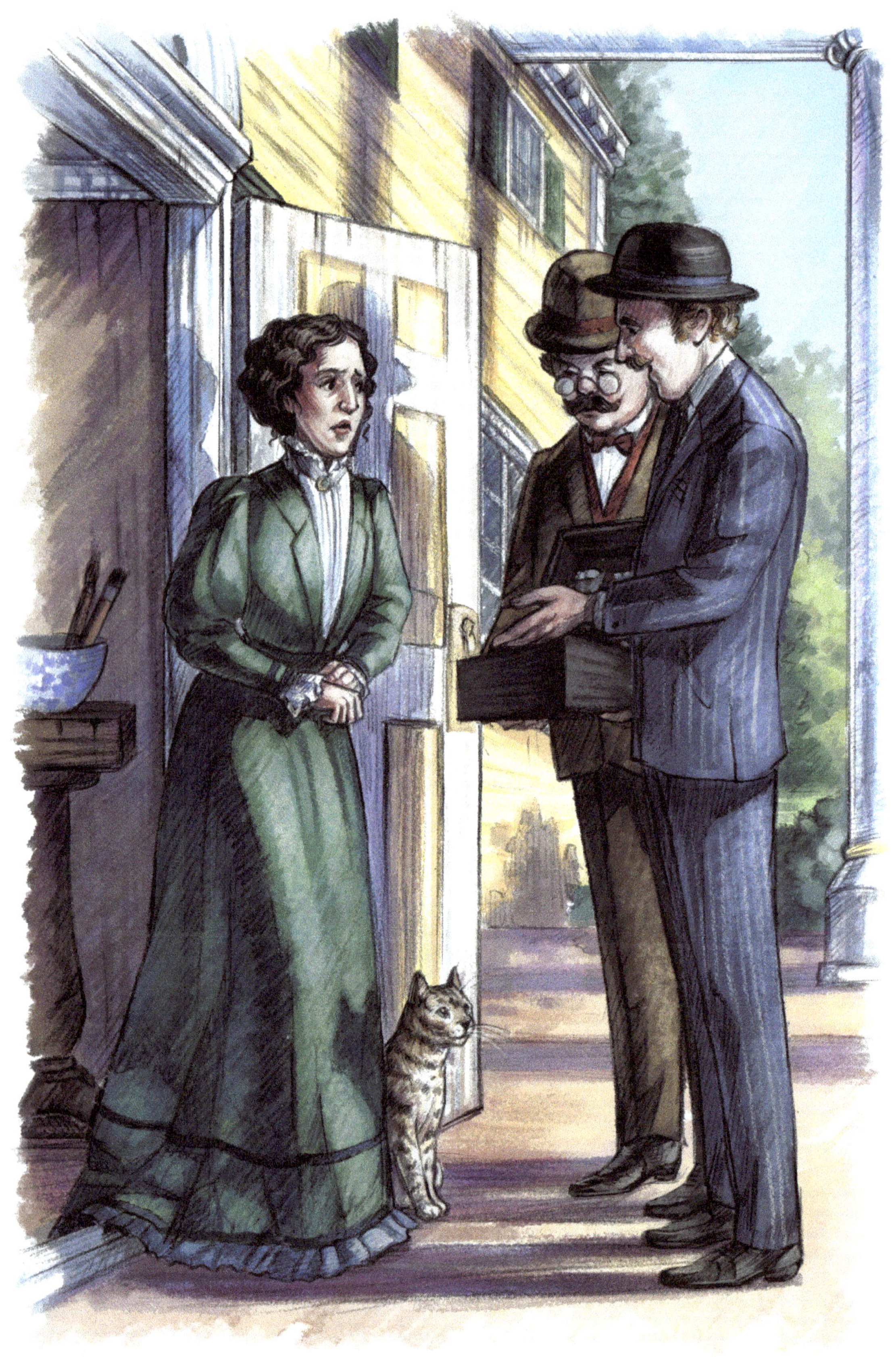

One year, as summer turned to fall and the house grew empty of artists, local merchants came knocking. They demanded Miss Florence pay her overdue bills. "What to do. What to do?" she sighed. Her many cats and a dog, two, or three, could not even comfort her.

Miss Florence knew with no money, she would be forced to leave her childhood home. It made her sick with worry.

She took to her bed, growing pale and weak.

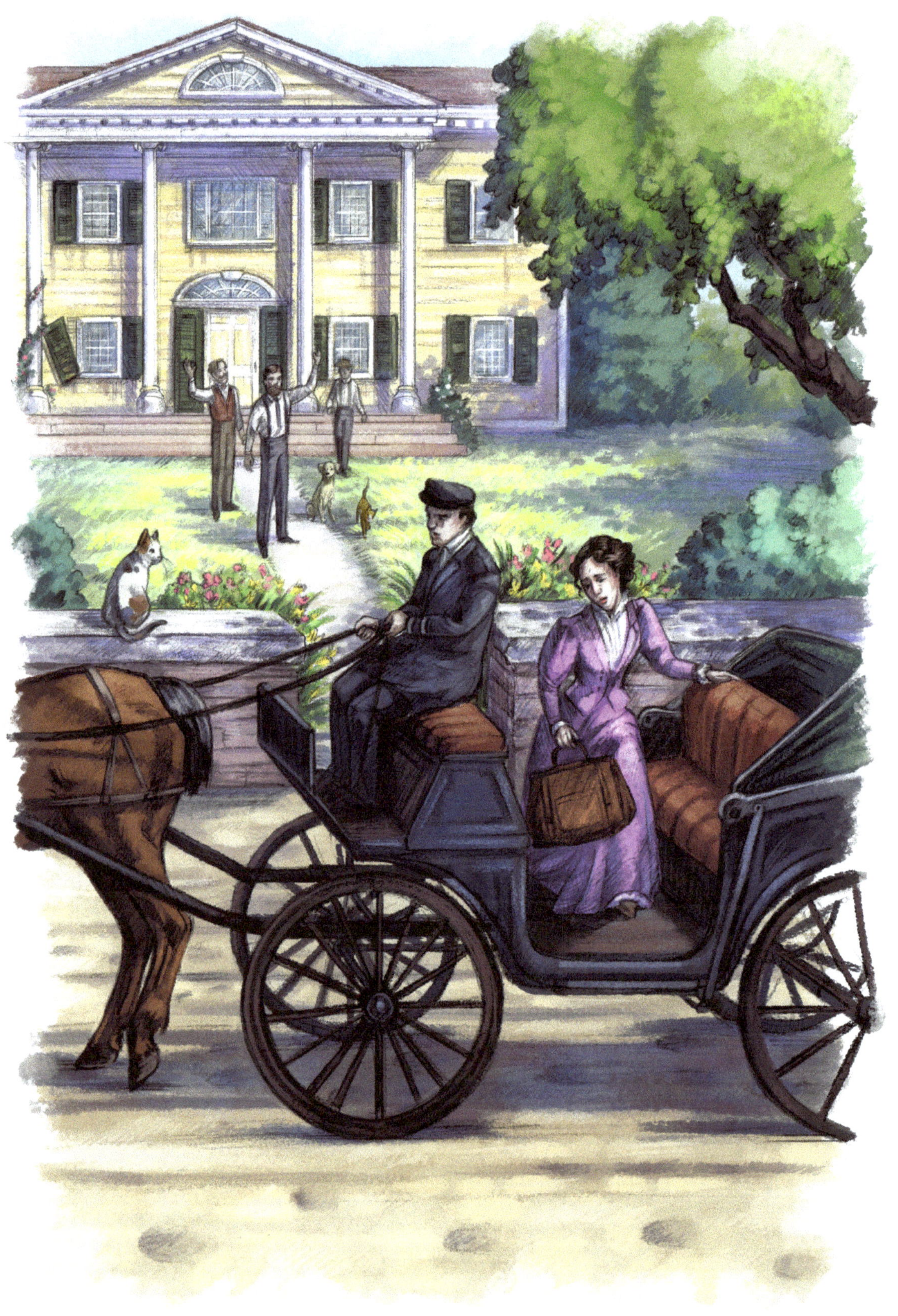

Soon, one of her artist-boarders got word so he rushed to the Griswold House and took action. He secretly sent letters to her friends in New York City and asked that they invite Miss Florence for a two-week getaway to clear her head. At first Miss Florence declined. She was just too beside herself. But then she reluctantly agreed, just barely making it into the carriage and off to the train station.

Little did she know that while she was away the artists had a plan. They knew Miss Florence, who had a heart big, wide, and welcoming, had friends far and wide. And so they spread the word. Things were dire. Funds came in faster than they ever imagined. Even future President Woodrow Wilson wife, the artist Ellen Axson Wilson, sent money to completely renovate two bedrooms. Because she, too, had spent summers at the beloved artist colony.

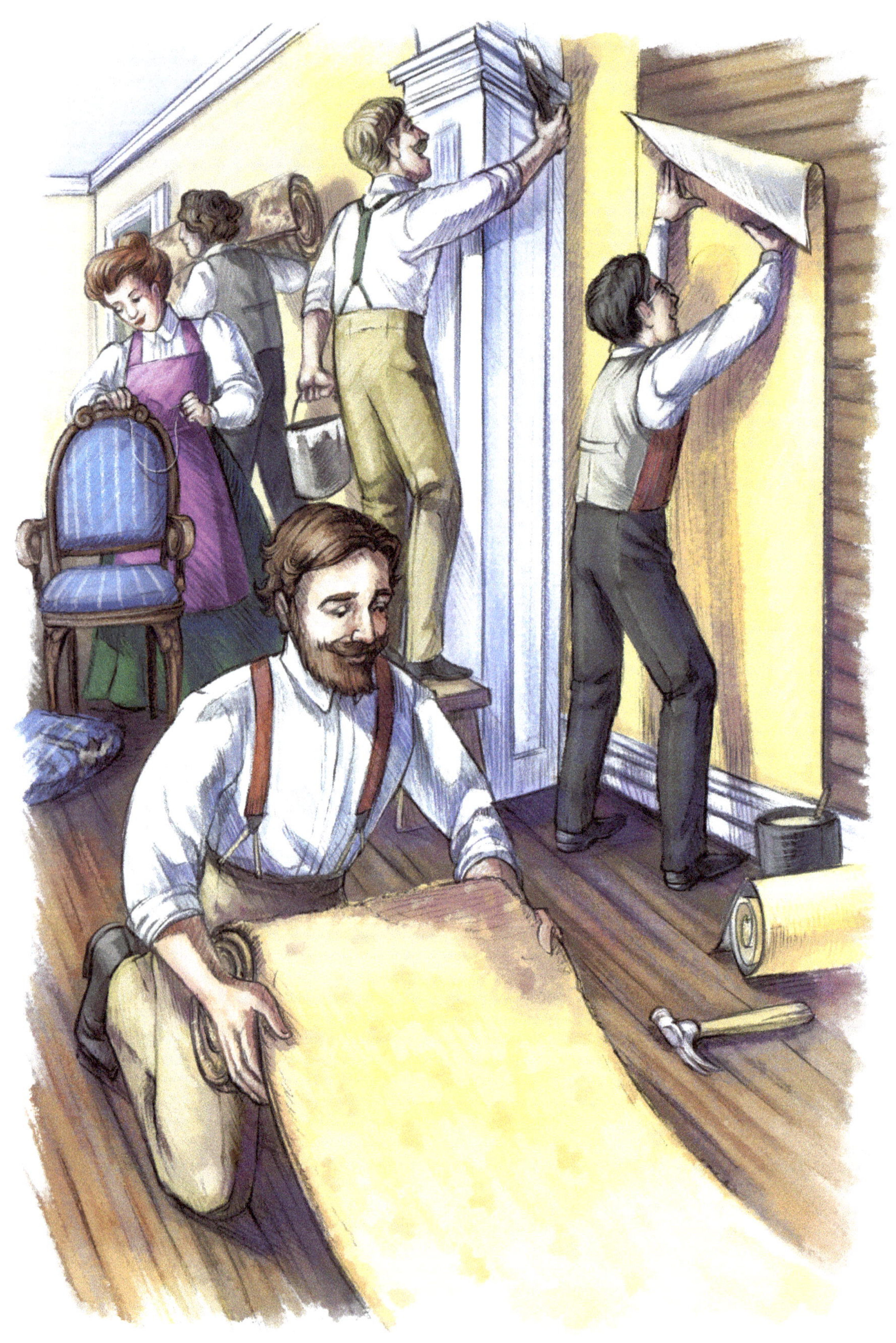

Artists from far and wide converged on Old Lyme, banding together in their usual rollicking style and got busy—fixing furniture, mending carpets, plastering ceilings, and painting inside and out. They hired masons, a plumber, electrician, adding hot and cold water. They eventually gave the Griswold House new life. And best of all, they paid off all of Miss Florence's over-due bills.

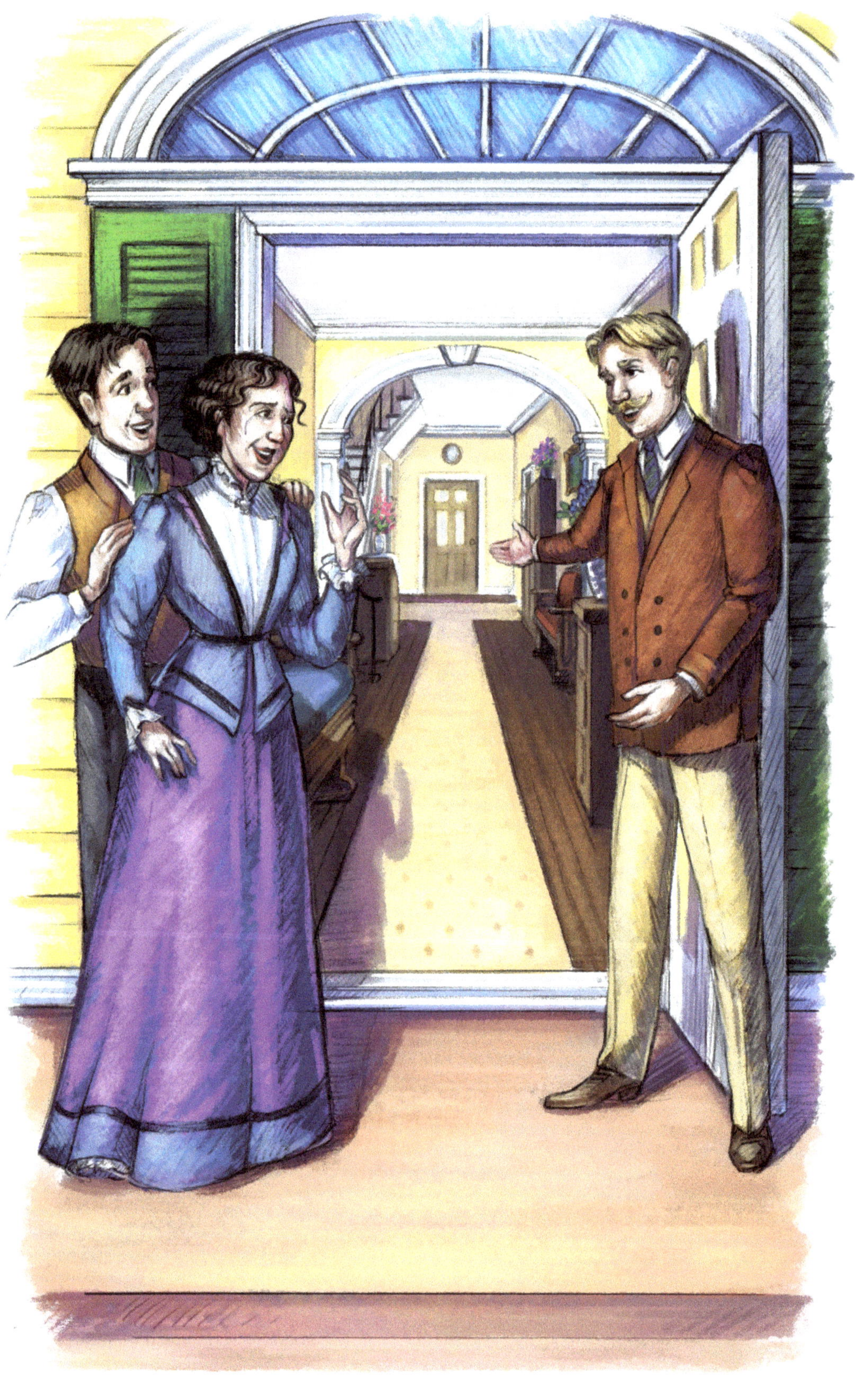

When Miss Florence returned home, she could hardly believe her eyes. Her beloved house sparkled anew. This was all beyond her wildest dreams. She cried tears of happiness.

From then on, Miss Florence who had a heart big, wide, and welcoming, along with her many cats and a dog, two or three, lived happily for many years.

"The Keeper of the Artist Colony," as she called herself, continued welcoming vacationing artists—all the while, unknowingly making history.

ABOUT THE AUTHOR

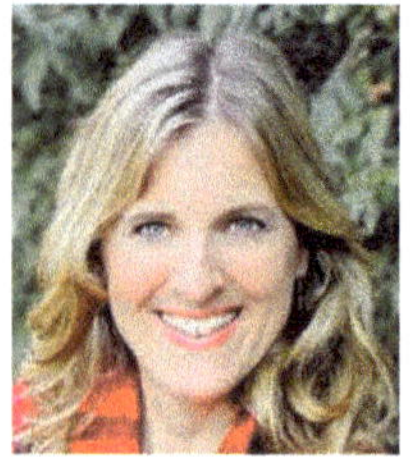
Deb Adamson

Deb writes on a wide variety of topics for children, from nonfiction picture book biographies that inspire, devotional stories that encourage, to rhyming and non-rhyming books, that make kids laugh. She is a member of the Society of Children's Book Writers and Illustrators (SCBWI). She lives on the shoreline of Connecticut with her husband, son and not a cat, two or three—but just one very special orange Tabby, named Lumpy. She has spent many memorable hours visiting the Florence Griswold Museum with her son. Visit her website at www.debadamson.com

ABOUT THE ILLUSTRATOR

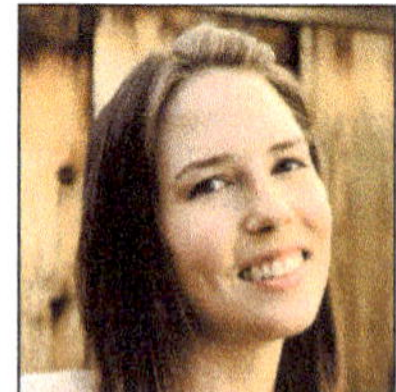
Anne Zimanski

Anne Zimanski is a freelance artist, specializing in children's book illustration. She has illustrated dozens of books in a wide range of styles and themes for publication across the United States and abroad. Anne is known as a versatile artist, well versed in both traditional and modern art techniques. Her illustrations often mix traditional mediums and aesthetics with modern digital painting styles, and have a focus on color and light play. Visit her website at www.annezimanski.com.

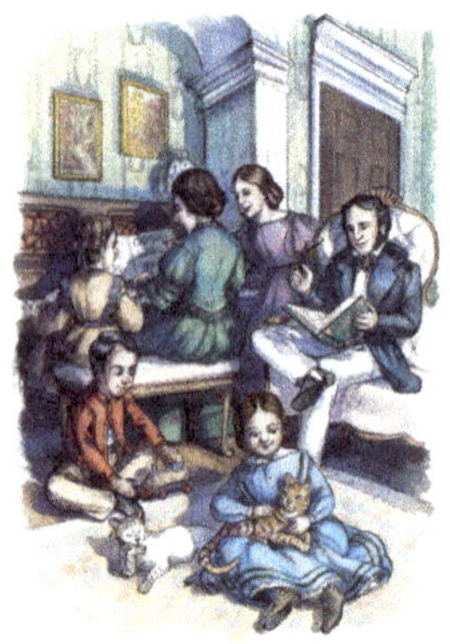

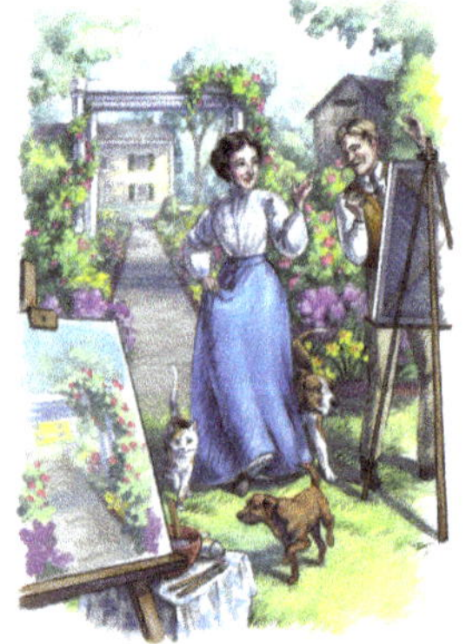

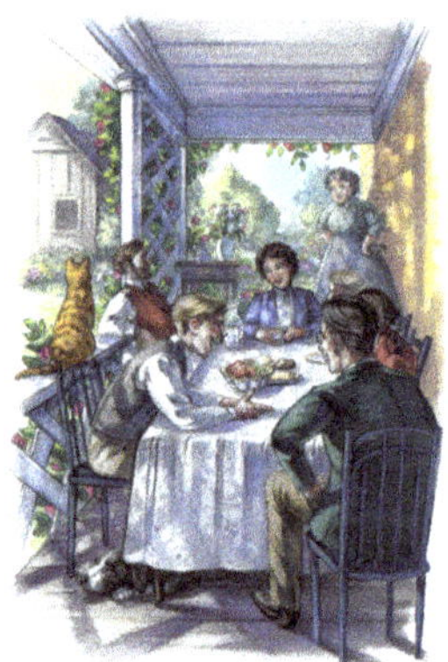

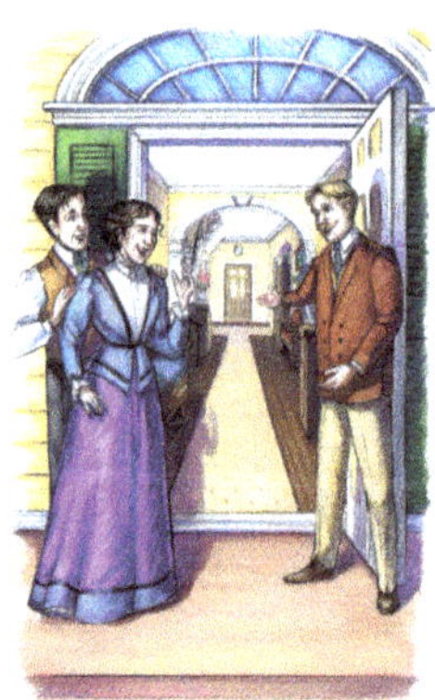

BIBLIOGRAPHY

The Florence Griswold Museum: www.florencegriswoldmuseum.org

Heming, Arthur, *Miss Florence and the Artists of Old Lyme*, 2nd Edition Florence Griswold Museum, 2013

www.ingramcontent.com/pod-product-compliance
Lightning Source LLC
LaVergne TN
LVHW060634110826
845147LV00014B/908